Brigitte Eilert-Overbeck

Kittens

Everything About Selection, Care, Nutrition, and Behavior

Filled with Full-color Photographs by Monika Wegler

BARRON'S

Contents

It Has to Be a Kitten

Soft, sweet angel and mischievous little devil with an inquisitive mind: a kitten embodies both and so conquers the human heart in a flash. This can be the beginning of a beautiful friendship . . .

The World of Cats

Cats are at home in two worlds. They have inherited one from their wild ancestors: the world of the hunter. They have to be quick and skillful, mastering the art of waiting and the lightning-fast attack. They need to know all the tricks in order to outsmart their prey, be ahead of their competitors, and escape from danger. Nature has also equipped cuddly little kittens with the weapons of their ancestors: sharp claws, a powerful bite, alertness, and highly developed senses. The kitten also has an agile, flexible body that Houdini would envy. Kittens are perfect predators, just like panthers, tigers, and other big cats.

The Kitten's Super Cat: Humans

Yet, the cat is also the perfect domesticated pet. Cats discovered their alternative world once humans started building houses. The human home means more to the cat than to any other animal: it is the *center* of its territory, an island of security, the found-again nursery, and indeed may be an earthly paradise. The human to whom a kitten has attached itself is more important to it than any other cat; for the domesticated cat that human is a "super cat"–the provider of warmth, affection, and food, just as the mother cat once did. Humans are companions with whom the kitten does not have to fight over food–or for prospective mates; and most certainly not over territory. Anyone who understands his or her cat leaves the sovereignty of the home to the cat and does not attempt to exert authority. In its own world, the cat is a hunter for whom command and obedience have no meaning; not even in our world, where the cat remains throughout its life always a child—a lovely child when it feels it is understood, but not always a well-behaved one.

Typical Cat!

Kittens are individualists. There are those that like to cuddle and those that prefer not to, the adventurers and the procrastinators, the energy bundles and the idle types. However, they all have some things in common:

› They enter into a lifelong partnership with humans for up to 20 years or more.

› They develop a close bond with the location where they live; it is their territory.

› They consider themselves in charge in the community of cats and humans.

› On the other hand, they consider their owners as "super cats" and mother substitutes from whom they expect a lot of attention.

› Cats are highly intelligent and, because of that, they are highly curious.

› They develop rituals and habits and don't like changes in their daily routine (e.g., traveling).

› They require a diet adapted to their needs and must be given regular care.

Is a Cat Really for Me?

A glance from innocent eyes, a shy *meow* and it has happened: a kitten has conquered a human heart. So that this love story has a happy ending, cool and calm consideration must also come into the equation. You should carefully review all the pros and cons; only then should you decide whether such an animal really suits you and fits into your life.

Responsibility. You will enter into a bond for life when you get a kitten. Do you have a clear head to make such a far-reaching decision? If your life is in some sort of turmoil (change of job, new partner, pending relocation), it's best to wait until your life has settled down again. At that point, you will be more relaxed and it will be easier for a kitten to start trusting you. Also, make sure there are no special problems that may prevent you from enjoying the company of a kitten. This may include an allergy to cats or landlord's rules that forbid keeping a cat in your house or apartment. Moreover, keep in mind that a kitten must be very much a part of your family life, and it should be welcomed by all family members.

Personal Space. Every cat needs its own territory, even when it will be an indoor-only cat. Cats need their own personal place, or—more precisely—several places: one for sleeping, one for feeding, and one for its litter box; in addition, several resting places and sites simply for withdrawing to.

A cute midget with gigantic paws: At this stage, the body proportions are not yet balanced.

Cuddling session: When a kitten nestles so trustingly in a child's arms, this is an enormous compliment to her little girlfriend. Obviously, the girl already understands a lot about the correct way to handle kittens.

There must also be places to play where they can climb and sharpen their claws, and an area to roam around in. Will you be able to provide the animal that much space, and are you willing to re-arrange your house or apartment to suit a cat?

Stubbornness. You cannot expect the cat to obey your every command, to submit to you, or to do behavioral tricks for you, unless (of course) the animal enjoys it. You will also have to live with the fact that sometimes the cat will sharpen its claws on

The **Scoundrels**

Even the cutest kittens are little scoundrels, and that is the way they often act. This requires not only training skill (see pages 50–51), but also considerable patience: at nine to 10 months, most kittens will settle down and become somewhat quieter.

Kittens Require More

	KITTEN	CAT
ENERGY	130 kcal/kg	80-100 kcal/kg
MEALS PER DAY	3–5	2
SLEEP	18–20 hours	Up to 16 hours
PLAY	Up to 2 hours	Up to 1 hour
REST PERIODS FROM PLAY	Plays until exhausted	Paces its play energy
GENTLENESS	Sensitive and still fragile	More robust
TRAINING	Will test limits	Knows established limits
TOLERANCE	Active	More subdued
SAFETY PRECAUTIONS	Courts danger because of innate curiosity	Usually cautious
RETREAT FACILITIES	Needs to familiarize itself with its territory	Has found favorite places

something it shouldn't, or it may simply occupy your favorite chair. Overall, kittens, with their innate charm, can cause a lot of havoc. Can you handle this without getting angry or striking the kitten?

Affection. Do you have a lot of time on your hands? Do you like to be at home? Cats need to have their owner around them; even more so little kittens. Not only early in the morning or late in the evening, but also a few hours during the day. They need to tell you what is on their mind (see Behavior Explained), rub against your legs, and ask for a bit of love and affection, or get you involved in some playing. A trusting relationship between human and cat can only develop through frequent physical contact and affection.

Curiosity. Imagination is in demand: Cats require stimuli that challenge their natural curiosity; on the other hand, kittens can get themselves into dangerous situations because of their unbridled drive to explore. Are you far-sighted enough to remove access to such risks before they can harm your kitten (see page 28–29)?

Consistency. With their lively temperament, kittens tend to cause all sorts of excitement. However, they are less than thrilled when their human masters do the same. Cats feel contented where things are quiet, consistent, and uneventful. They do not long for a change in scenery. Do you have someone on hand who will reliably look after and care for the cat when you go on vacation, get sick, or need to go somewhere for a while?

Food and Care. A cat will cost you money. Are you willing to pay about $750 per year for food, litter, veterinary expenses, and other small extras? One more consideration: Would an adult cat be better suited for you than an active, demanding kitten? There are mature cats that are past the rambunctious kitten phase waiting in animal shelters.

An Addition to the Family

Does anyone object to a new family member with fur and paws? If not, the time has come for a few further points to consider:

Child and Kitten. They could be a dream team! Yet, the kitten can feel overwhelmed by youthful exuberance, and improper handling can lead to injuries for both kitten and child. Therefore, your child should be of school age when you bring a kitten into the family and must be taught how to handle a kitten. The child should willingly participate in looking after the new family member. However, even if the child wholeheartedly wanted a kitten as a pet, he or she cannot fully understand the responsibility connected with such a pet. Consequently, kitten care will remain on your shoulders.

One Kitten or Two? One kitten is good; two are better! In each litter, there are siblings that play with each other more than with the other siblings. A kitten that has a pal in the same litter will settle down in a new home quicker, the two will not get bored in your absence, and they will keep each other fit. Of course, both together can add up to twice the mischief; however, a single kitten may turn your home upside-down simply because it is bored.

Female or Male? Female cats are considered more gentle and affectionate, but they can also be more stubborn than males; on the other hand, male cats may play rougher, but also can be friendlier than females. However, since kittens are born individualists, for the time being you can ignore these small differences. Moreover, unless you want to become a pedigreed cat breeder, you will need to get your cat (or cats) neutered or spayed later on anyway.

There Is Already a Cat in the House. You may be getting a kitten to keep your older cat company. In principle, this is not a bad idea, because a kitten will adjust quicker than a fully grown cat and is more likely to be accepted. Nevertheless, initially the older one is not going to be thrilled. You will need to have patience to get both of them adjusted to each other (see pages 34–35).

Together we are irresistible: a two-kitten team will conquer its new human family in a short period.

If your cat has already reached senior age as a soloist, or its health is no longer the best, you may want to put off such a plan. A kitten would only add stress.

Dog and Cat. They are not arch enemies. As a rule, a well-trained dog will generally accept a kitten and even want to protect it. However, misunderstandings can arise from the different languages of the two; for instance, dogs raise a paw when they want to play, but cats threaten claw strikes with a raised paw. Yet, when you cleverly mediate between the two (see pages 34–35), you can prevent such communication problems.

Cats and Other Pets. With a lot of patience, you can accustom large rabbits to a kitten, but you had better not leave them alone together. Guinea pigs, hamsters, rats, dwarf rabbits, and birds are not comfortable in the presence of cats. These animals fit too well into the scheme of being prey for the hunter cat—and they know it. Therefore, it is not a good idea to put a kitten into a small pet menagerie (see pages 34–35).

Roaming Freely or Indoor Cat? In good conscience you can only permit your cat to roam outdoors where there is no car traffic or no wildlife nearby, and the neighbors have no problem with cats. If you live in an urban area, your kitten will live years longer if it stays indoors. Otherwise, as a compromise, you can provide an outdoor run within a securely fenced-off area in your backyard or in a large outdoor (aviary-type) cage with a cat door into the house. However, even living in an apartment and without outdoor access, you can make a stimulating feline environment (see pages 54–55). A kitten that has not been exposed to the outdoors during its formative period (third to seventh week of its life), will never miss the dangers of roaming in the wild.

The little indoor kitten needs lots of stimulation. The owner needs to make sure that boredom does not become a problem.

Two Kittens—One Temperament

A KITTEN THAT IS ALWAYS INDOORS will be bored when you go off to work. The best solution: instead of one kitten, take two from the same litter (see page 9). However, you can reduce adjustment and compatibility problems if you get a companion for your kitten at some later stage.

THE SECOND KITTEN should have a similar temperament to the first one: one brash little kitten is best matched up with another mischievous one. On the other hand, an aggressive kitten can easily intimidate a shy kitten. The respective sex is not important here: male, female, or mixed pairs that have been together from the earliest stage usually get along well later on, too.

How the Cat Became What It Is Now

Mice in Middle Eastern countries followed humans into houses for grain and other edible supplies. The African Wild Cat (*Felis silvestris libyca*) in turn followed them. More and more of these cats changed their hunting habits to prey on the mice that lived in human habitats, and so became the ancestors of our domesticated cat. Humans, for their part, realized how helpful cats were at ridding the foodstores of rodents, and then found that cats made wonderful companions, too.

From Egypt to the Whole World

Ancient Egyptians, 6,000 to 4,000 years ago, were already breeding cats. Despite feline export prohibitions, the descendants of the African Wild Cat moved out into the whole world and gradually adapted to their respective new environments. In Southeast Asia a slender, shorthair breed evolved— the ancestral forms of the Siamese and Burmese cats. In the rough and rugged highlands of Asia Minor, the first longhair cats appeared as the ancestors of present day Persian cats and those breeds with medium-long hair. Cats in temperate zones developed a more compact body and denser short fur with an insulating undercoat: the original European shorthair cat. When ships traveled to the New World, cats went along and populated the North American continent.

Among the Egyptians, cats were considered holy, representations of Bastet (Bast), the goddess of sensual pleasure and domestic happiness. Cats had a similar sacred status associated with the Sun god Ra and the goddess Isis. During the late Middle Ages, leaders of the Christian faith declared cats to be allies of the devil, and consequently persecuted cats relentlessly for hundreds of years. Nowadays, the cat plays a role among humans that's far more suited to it: wonderful companion and purring soulmate.

Well camouflaged among leaves: just like thousands of years ago, the little predator still likes to hunt rodents as prey.

Abyssinian
Intelligent and obstinate

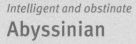

This old breed came from Abyssinia (now Ethiopia) and was transported to Great Britain.

Appearance/impression. Abyssinians are of medium size; they are slender and long-legged, with a relatively narrow head, large ears, and green to gold-colored eyes. They have a short dense fur with characteristic "ticking," i.e., individuals have alternating light and dark bands. Best known is the original (ruddy) variety—a mini-cougar.

Temperament/character. The Abyssinian cat has its own mind and gets its own way with charm and intelligence. Its constant state of activity sometimes causes the animal to react as if frightened; therefore, it may take some time until a kitten gains sufficient trust in you and its new surroundings. Yet, once it has embraced a human emotionally, it is very affectionate. These cats demand a lot of attention, but at the same time, they like to be independent. If an outdoor run is not available for this cat, you will need to provide a lot of stimulation and activity in your home.

British Shorthair
Uncomplicated and well-balanced

The origin of this breed is England; the ancestors are British housecats and Persians.

Appearance/impression. Their owners often refer to British Shorthair cats as "little bears." These cats have a good-natured charisma, a plush-like coat that is slightly raised off the body, and a harmonious roundness. The most popular color is the British Blue, although the breed comes in many other colors. Its fur has a silvery blue sheen, and the large, round eyes are copper- or orange-colored. The British Shorthair cat now comes in many of the color and pattern varieties known in Persians.

Temperament/character. British Shorthair cats have a mellow temperament. They get along with singles as well as with families.

Curious and sociable
Burmese

The origin of this breed is in Burma (now Myanmar); however, the breed as we know it today was first bred in the United States, through crossbreeding with Siamese.

Appearance/impression. The Burmese cat has short, smooth, silky-shiny fur on head, back, and legs, somewhat darker than the abdomen. Two types of body exist in the US. The Extreme has a round head, a full face, a short broad muzzle, and a visible nose break. The Traditional's head is moderately wedge-shaped with rounded lines, and the nose has a less pronounced "stop." Both have large, golden-yellow to amber-colored eyes.

Temperament/character. The Burmese cat is similar in temperament and affinity for people to the Siamese cat, but is not as demanding. This cat is equally comfortable in the company of other cats. It does not like being left alone. Among its prominent characteristics is its curiosity—possibly a reason why this cat is easier to take along in a car than other cats.

Robust and sociable
Maine Coon

The name of this large, powerful, and robust cat has nothing to do with raccoons ("coons"). It developed in the state of Maine, and presumably originated from a cross between native cats and long-haired cats brought into the country by sailors.

Appearance/Impression. Semi-long hair, particularly dense during the winter, and bushy, raccoon-like tail, with tufts of hair on the tips of the ears like the lynx. These cats have a friendly disposition, and, in contrast to their body size, their voice is delicate and soft.

Temperament/character. Maine Coon cats get along well with other animals, but they also enjoy human company and adapt well to a family with children. They are not necessarily a lap cat, but instead prefer to play and can even be interested in retrieving. They are enthusiastic hunters that love to pounce on a catnip mouse.

In for a cuddle and adventurous

Norwegian Forest Cat

This is the cat that came in from the cold; more precisely, from the cold climatic zones of Scandinavia. Just like the Maine Coon, the Norwegian Forest cat also developed naturally through random crossbreeding of long- and shorthaired cats.

Appearance/impression. Over the course of time, the Norwegian has developed into a rough and tough all-weather cat, with a powerful, robust body and semi-long, "double" fur—water-repellent outer hair and a warm undercoat. It has a triangular head, large ears with tufts of hair, a magnificent neck frill, and "britches" on its hind legs.

Temperament/character. Its favorite adventure includes climbing; its specialty is climbing down a cat tree.....headfirst! Norwegian Forest cats are very sociable, playful, and cuddly; they prefer active affection to quiet lap sessions.

Calm and majestic

Persian

Persians are the descendants of "Angora cats," the name for all longhaired breeds hundreds of years ago, which were popular with the nobility.

Appearance/Impression. The long, silky fur flows around the body of the Persian Cat, very much like an imperial robe. This cat is large and has a strong, stocky body with short, sturdy legs. The tail is bushy and somewhat short. The small, slightly rounded ears nearly disappear in the lush fur of the head and neck. The head is large and round, and the large, shiny eyes are typical, as is the wide, small pug nose with a "stop" or "break" (the indentation in the transition to the forehead). There are hundreds of color and pattern varieties of Persian cats.

Temperament/character. These little society lions have a calm temperament and are more likely to be lap cats than exercise fanatics. They can be very affectionate and love to be gently brushed and combed; regular grooming is essential so that their "imperial robes" do not become matted.

Gentle and very compatible

Ragdoll

This breed was developed in California in the 1960s. It's not known what pedigreed cats, if any, were its ancestors.

Appearance/impression. Ragdolls are "heavy-weights" among cats, often weighing 15 to 20 pounds. Ragdolls have a large, wedge-shaped head, bright blue eyes, semi-long, very silky fur, and four white "gloves."

Temperament/character. Ragdoll cats are not temperamental, and adults are calm and relaxed. They enjoy attention and company, but never become insistent. They get along well with children and are generally compatible with other animals. Their name comes from the characteristic that when picked up, the cat will relax with its body hanging down limp...just like a ragdoll. They are ideal for a life indoors.

Temperamental and sensible

Siamese

Originally, Siamese cats came from Thailand, but they have been bred in Europe for more than 130 years now, and in North America for more than 100.

Appearance/impression. European and American Siamese varieties have become far removed from their Thai ancestors. They are now more slender and graceful, the once roundish head is now wedge-shaped, and the fur has become shorter, smoother, and finer. The bright blue eyes remained. Siamese cats are partial albinos, born white, with the final permanent color of the fur emerging gradually, along with the characteristic dark markings (the "points") on the head, ears, tail, legs, and paws.

Temperament/character. Siamese cats are for con-noisseurs. They take over their owner completely, and always want to be kept busy. With their remark-ably strong voice, they always have something to *say*. They learn quickly and can be taught a number of behaviors, and so place demands on their owner even when playing.

Welcome to Life!

Two to three times a year female cats come into heat. This is a period of extreme attraction between female and male cats; normally, mating is followed by pregnancy. This will last about 65 days, but it can vary by a few days either way. For the forthcoming birth, the female will look for a protected "nest"—ideally in a prepared box. Within a few hours, the female will give birth to three to five young, sometimes more. As soon as a kitten is born, its mother will free it from the fetal membrane and lick it dry. Subsequently she will eat the afterbirth and chew off the umbilical cord down to a short remnant. After having given birth to the kittens, the female will lie down along one side of them to nurse them while her body forms a protective wall around them. For the first four weeks, the female will totally look after the young, including providing "diaper service": following nursing, the mother will lick the kittens' genitals to stimulate them to urinate and defecate.

The First Few Weeks

A newborn kitten weighs about 3.5 ounces; it cannot see, can barely hear, and has only a thin baby fur coat. The legs are suitable only for crawling but are used for this immediately. Guided by its tactile and olfactory perception only, the kitten crawls towards the maternal milk source. It uses the front paws for massaging the nipples in order to enhance the flow of milk. With the initial mother's milk, the colostrum, the kittens receive important antibodies that give them protection against infections for a period of about eight weeks. Their voices cannot yet produce a full "meow"; instead, vocalization consists of high-pitched squeaking and whimpering. This signals to the mother: "*I need you.*" The young are also able to hiss if there is something they do not like.

Lightweight: The mother transports the young by means of a neck grip, while the young go limp.

Daily Progress

During the first two weeks, life for the kittens consists exclusively of nursing and sleeping. It makes sense that the young at that stage can only barely move: after all, they are not yet able to regulate their own body temperature. If they were able to move around independently, they could easily become too cold or too hot. When the mother goes away for a short period, all the kittens in the litter will move—with a lot of kicking—into a "cuddle huddle." There each kitten will try very hard to get to the most desirable position on the bottom of the huddle; on top of it, the nest heat quickly dissipates. Even though initially it may not look like it, the little kittens make daily progress. No more than four days after birth, the kittens will purr while nursing; from the fifth day on, they show reaction to sounds. During the second week, their ears become erect and they are able to recognize where a particular sound is coming from. Between the seventh and twelfth day, their initially pale blue eyes will open, but vision is still limited. The milk teeth develop, the first being the incisor teeth. Initial attempts to stand on their legs towards the end of the second week are still wobbly, but the kittens are then already able to extend and retract their claws and to hold onto something when they lose their balance.

Formative Period: Toward the end of the second week the first formative phase begins: the experiences the kitten has now will mold its personality and future behavior. From the third week on,

Developmental Phases of a Kitten

	1ST TO 4TH WEEK	5TH TO 9TH WEEK	10TH TO 14TH WEEK
WEIGHT	3.5 oz–18 oz	21 oz–33 oz	35 oz–60 oz
SENSES	Hearing perfect at fourth week. Visual orientation at third week.	Vision and locomotion improve; posture reflex at fifth week.	Locomotion and sense of balance perfect, vision perfect at twelfth week.
BODY	Eyes opening, ears stand erect, first milk teeth. Claws can be withdrawn at second week; improved movement coordination at third week; independent elimination at fourth week.	Incisors appear, complete milk teeth at sixth week, stable body temperature at seventh week. Males gain substantially more weight and size than females at ninth week.	Eyes permanently colored, movement and coordination perfect at tenth week; dentition changes at thirteenth week.
BEHAVIOR & CAPABILITIES	Drinking, sleeping; purring at fourth day; first attempts to walk at second week; first leaps at third week; first excursions from the nest at fourth week.	Increased curiosity, climbing, catching games at fifth week; "cat washing" at sixth week; playing with objects at seventh week; weaning.	At tenth week perfect jumping and balancing; at twelfth week less competitive playing; interest in hunting increased.

The Formative Phase

TIPS FROM
CAT EXPERT
Brigitte Eilert-Overbeck

EARLY PRACTICE. All the things a kitten learns at this early age will not frighten it later on. This is particularly important for the formative phases from the fourth to the seventh week, which is also the stage during which socialization begins.

KEEPING GOOD COMPANY FROM THE START. Some breeders make sure during this period that their kittens have positive experiences with several adults, children, other cats, and friendly dogs. Here kittens also become familiar with things and situations which they will later have to handle.

FIRST EXPERIENCES. For instance, kittens should be encouraged to explore the cat carrier, in order to start getting acquainted with the inevitable trips to the veterinarian (it is advisable for the first exam to take place during the fourth week), or the kittens may even take part in a brief car trip. This will not only spare the kitten a lot of trauma—but also its new human family when the actual time comes to visit the veterinarian later on.

progress becomes easier to recognize. Although the little ones are still somewhat shaky on their legs, they will attempt the first cat pounces, arching their backs and fluffing their tails. Their listening capacity and vision steadily improve; the kittens are now able to visually recognize their mother and siblings, and search for their mother's nipples using their eyes rather than just their nose. The process of socialization also starts in the course of this formative phase. From the mother and siblings, as well as from other cats in the household, the kitten learns how it is supposed to interact with other cats. During the fourth through eighth weeks of their life, kittens find it particularly easy to become friends with humans, provided they have pleasant experiences. Therefore, it is very important to provide friendly encounters with adults and children in the kitten's first home. In addition, positive contacts with dogs or other animals can contribute much to the kitten becoming an uncomplicated household member.

Exploring its World. During the fourth week a kitten's hearing is fully developed. The little ones attempt the first excursions from the nest and may even sample a bit of food from the mother's food dish. Cat mothers with outdoor access may bring in the first prey. Gradually, the mother is winding down the "diaper service"; by then, the kittens will have learned how to use the litter box. This works better with every passing day. From the fifth week on—at the latest—the kittens are being nursed noticeably less and will require some additional solid food daily. Meanwhile, the eyes have turned bright blue and vision has improved even more. The kittens are now more agile and engage in some risky climbing and jumping for a good reason: by this time the "posture reflex"—the ability to

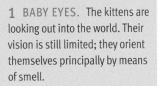

1 BABY EYES. The kittens are looking out into the world. Their vision is still limited; they orient themselves principally by means of smell.

2 OPEN FOR IMPRESSIONS. At an age of four weeks, the formative phase has begun: impressions and experiences gained at that stage will form the basis of their subsequent behavior.

3 DISCOVERING NEW TERRITORY. While playing, the 10-week old kitten learns. With 12 to 16 weeks, it is able to "conquer" its new family.

land on its feet—has fully developed. Six-week-old kittens scurry around, climb, and leap about. They have a complete set of milk teeth and can clean their fur as well as adult cats. Their body temperature remains relatively stable from the seventh week onward. The little cats are now more active, wrestle with their siblings, and play with everything that comes their way. Towards the end of the eighth week, the mother gradually stops nursing the young, but that does not terminate her influence: whatever mother likes best will also become the young's favorite food. The immune protection provided to the young by their mother's milk also comes to an end—time for an examination by the veterinarian and the first immunizations (see page 43).

Learning for Life

At the age of 10 weeks, a kitten has its permanent eye color—unless the kitten is Siamese or another breed with blue eyes, the eyes change color, usually to yellow, orange, or green. It is as agile as a high-wire performer and has all the skills required for hunting; however, learning social skills within the family unit has not yet been completed. Kittens at that age love to play; they learn with the greatest of ease, copying the behavior of adult cats, from a friendly encounter to a hostile conflict. With this, and through interactions with their mother, they learn the finer points of cat language. For instance, they are able to communicate who has the higher status, how to avoid fights, and how one comes to terms with other cats. Almost any kitten who has had such training can integrate into a new family without any problems.

By 12 weeks (16 weeks at the very latest), the kittens will have learned nearly everything. Their vision is fully developed and playing with siblings is less frequent: stalking, pursuing, and capturing "prey" (e.g., catnip mice) is far more interesting! Gradually, the milk teeth are replaced by permanent teeth; however, kittens do not obtain their complete adult teeth until they are six months old. In the meantime, the kitten should have been fully vaccinated and so be ready for its new life: a territory awaits the little discoverer. And people to love. . . .

Physical Equipment of a Kitten

Tail

When jumping, cats use their tail as a rudder to make sure they land correctly and for balancing. The tail is also a mood barometer and a device for communication.

Ears

Cats can hear sounds that we cannot even perceive, especially in the high-frequency range. Since a cat can also rotate its ears by almost 280 degrees, it is also very easy for the animal to determine where a particular sound is coming from.

Paws

Their well-padded soles and toes give cats the ability to walk without making a sound. These pads also serve as shock absorbers and braking mechanisms, and they also house a weapon arsenal: The front paws are equipped with five claws each, and the hind paws with four claws. So that the claws are not worn down or dulled while walking, they retract into skin pockets called "sheaths." The claws extend for climbing, fighting, or holding on. The cat must sharpen them regularly.

Eyes

Cats can see well spatially (in three dimensions) and so are able to estimate distances. Because of a reflective layer of cells behind the retina called the tapetum lucidum, the little hunter sees well at night.

Nose

The sense of smell is hardly used by cats for the detection of prey, but more for examining food and communication. When two cats meet for the first time, they start out by smelling each other. The tip of the nose is also a heat sensor: the cat uses it to test the temperature of an object before touching it with its paws.

Whiskers

Around the mouth, above the eyes, and along the back of the front paws there are sensory or tactile hairs— the cat's radar. The cat uses them to make the initial physical contact with the environment. With these whiskers, a cat senses the slightest air turbulence around it and receives tactile stimuli and can thus avoid obstacles in the dark.

A Great Team

The decision has been made—a kitten is moving in. This will be exciting for both you and your animal! If you know the kitten's peculiarities, you can save yourself and the new family member many unnecessary hassles right from the start.

Falling in Love—Cautiously

Is there much to think about once you have decided to get a kitten? Actually, there's quite a lot! After all, you want the new "roomie" to be healthy and to quickly start to trust you so it will fit into the family without undue delay, and so there will not be major training problems. Finally, you want the new family member to be happy with you and your home. With that in mind, first of all a warning: do not immediately fall in love with the very first kitten you come across. Unfortunately, such advice is equally difficult to heed.

Finding a kitten is not difficult. In the spring, humane associations and animal shelters have many more kittens than potential homes. It's better to consider a shelter than a "free to good home" ad, because shelter kittens are usually examined by a veterinarian and will be neutered before being placed. You must pay a fee for these services, but the price is less than if you took the kitten to the vet yourself. Also, the shelter workers are trained to recognize health and behavior problems. At a shelter there is less danger that "love at first sight" will blind you to possible problems. Moreover, with a free kitten there are more dangers that after a few weeks you will tumble painfully down from cloud nine.

Kittens from Good Homes Only!

It is better to learn as much as you can about a particular kitten's background before you make a decision that will last for the duration of the cat's life! Shelters often have information that will help you decide. If everything is all right (see pages 24–25) and you have a good feeling about it, you can start preparation for the new family member moving in (see page 26).

Buying a Pedigreed Cat from a Breeder

It goes without saying that a kitten is not a piece of merchandise. Therefore, breeders refer to a "negotiated arrangement" or "placement" of their protégés. Anyway, whatever you want to call it, there are a few rules you need to keep in mind.

Home Rule. If possible, visit the cattery where the cat was bred. Make sure the kittens were raised "underfoot," and where they have constant contact with people. This way your kitten moves from the warmth and security of one home to that of another home and so already has basic trust in humans.

Information Rule. Never omit the on-site visit, even if the breeder offers to bring the kitten over. This way you can see for yourself how the breeder interacts with his or her cats, and whether the cats are shy or friendly. Look for signs that the kittens were raised with the proper affection and stimuli, such as cat toys and scratching posts.

The "Gut Feeling" Rule. Look elsewhere for a kitten if you are not absolutely convinced that the animals are being raised in a loving environment; if you don't you may have to prepare yourself for a difficult tenant.

The "Breed Rule." Hands off kittens from backyard breeders. Most of these are from breeders who are not members of breeder associations, and who are not bound by strict guidelines regarding such things as mating frequency and health monitoring. Addresses of respectable breeders can be provided by the various cat associations (see page 62). These breeders cannot offer low prices, but can provide you with a kitten that is typical for the breed, healthy, and is well socialized.

Delivery Rule. Even though you may be able to select your kitten much earlier, it should remain with its mother until at least the twelfth week. Most breeders won't release their kittens any earlier, and some wait until 16 weeks. This is not only important for its development (see pages 16–19), but also for its continued health. This way the kitten is given a

So relaxed in the cat carrier? No problem! You find out how to achieve that on page 42.

timely health check and receives its first immuniza-tion (see pages 42–43) against infectious diseases while still in its original home.

The Kitten Must Be Healthy

A kitten that is healthy and has been immunized can be spared the visit to the veterinarian during the first few weeks in your home. Therefore, watch for the following points:

› Curious, interested behavior
› Fluffy, silky fur without knots and mats
› Clear, shiny eyes and slightly moist nose without any discharge, as well as clean, odorless ears
› White teeth and coral-pink gums
› A taut, firm body with a soft, but not bloated belly
› Clean anal region without signs of fecal matter

When a Kitten Needs Help

An unwanted kitten—especially during the spring and summer months—often ends up in an animal shelter. You are doing a good deed if you decided on a kitten from a shelter. The kittens are immu-nized and will not be put up for adoption unless they are healthy. But what if a motherless stray or a "dumped" kitten comes across your path? Such cats can make wonderful companions. However, the cat may need love and patience before it will trust you. It's possible such a kitten will never become well-adjusted. Moreover, such an animal must be kept isolated until it is immunized, is free of any parasites, and a veterinarian has determined that it is not suffering from contagious diseases (see pages 44–45).

Properly Raised Pedigreed Kittens

TIPS FROM
CAT EXPERT
Brigitte Eilert-Overbeck

The following points indicate that your pedigreed kitten comes from a "good stable":

THE KITTEN moves about in its new home, full of curiosity, and is completely uninhibited.

THE BREEDER or cat owner, respectively, has a personal relationship with each of his or her ani-mals and shares the home with them.

IN THE KITTEN'S HOME, there is no evidence of skimping on food, care, or health.

FEEDING AND SLEEPING SITES, as well as lit-ter boxes, are clean and hygienic.

ALL ANIMALS are free of parasites, and there are complete immunization records when the kit-ten is handed over.

A SALES CONTRACT IS INDICATED—a good breeder will not hand over a pedigreed kitten without the proper registration papers and a vet-erinary health certificate.

THE BREEDER OR CAT OWNER will want to know what becomes of his or her animals, and will take time to answer all your questions.

Basic Equipment Needed for a Kitten

First, we need a transport carrier made of hard plastic with a solid floor. If the kitten gets sick during transport or needs to "go to the toilet," everything can easily be cleaned up again. Thereafter, the same box is essential for visits to the veterinarian (see pages 42–43). During car travel, the box must always be properly secured!

1 Everything for beauty care

In terms of "beauty utensils," you will need (depending on the length and undercoat of the fur) a metal comb and a brush; for very shorthaired animals a glove with a knobbed surface may do. For longhaired cats, you will also require a mat-removing tool called a matbreaker to cut out matted knots of hair. Combs with rotating teeth do not pull on hair as much. A flea comb is useful as well.

2 Serving the meal!

A cat's "table" consists of a washable mat and a bowl for dry and wet food per each cat, preferably of ceramic or stainless steel; plastic bowls eventually start to crack, become unhygienic, and can contribute to feline acne. A water bowl should be a few feet away from the feeding site; domestic cats wander over to their "watering hole" only after they have completed their meal. You can also offer a container of fresh cat grass; sprouted winter wheat is good for digestion and easy to grow.

3 For sweet dreams

The kitten will usually find its own favorite sleeping place; keep a bed, blanket, and pillow handy, to place them wherever the kitten prefers to rest.

4 There must be toys

Little balls, mice made of cloth or fake fur, little toys with catnip—anything that moves and can be tossed, that is neither sharp-edged nor very pointed and cannot be swallowed, is welcome as a toy. Avoid painted toys made in China, since the paint usually contains lead, which is fatal to kittens and even full-grown cats.

5 The litter box

Two litter boxes are better than one; with two cats, it is advisable to have three such facilities. Some cats distinguish between a place for urinating and another one for defecating. Some cats do not like to use litter boxes that have been used by another cat. Small kittens prefer litter boxes with a low rim (four inches). Later on, you can change over to a larger box, so active burrowers will not scatter a lot of litter over the edge of the box.

6 Always central: the scratching post

A nice large scratching post or an equivalent scratching facility is required even if the kitten has access to trees that have thick bark. Sharpening the claws serves not only to improve body condition and remove dead nail flakes, but is also for marking the territory. If no cat tree is available, the cat will scratch carpet or furniture. The scratching post must be large enough that even an adult cat can stretch itself on it, and it must be secure! A model with sisal rope for scratching and platforms and tubes for playing and resting is ideal.

Ready for the Reception—Final Preparations

The big event requires proper preparations. Take a few days off for the arrival of the kitten—a weekend is the absolute minimum—for the big event. Rest assured, the time spent will not seem long!

The Reception Room. Eventually the entire home will belong to your kitten, maybe with the exception of your bedroom if you'd rather keep the cat out of your sleeping area. Initially the newly arrived animal will feel very uneasy and may hide under a couch or a dresser—especially when there are a lot of activities in the home, even though these may well be normal family activities. Therefore, if possible, set up a single room for the animal as a reception hall. There you place the cat bed in a protected corner that gives the kitten a good view of the entire room. Also put the cat's food bowl, as well as the water bowl and the litter box, in this room. The latter should be sufficiently far away from the bed and the feeding site. For sharpening the claws in the reception hall, an economic temporary scratch-

Best vantage point: From the windowsill, the kitten has an overview of the entire room, and to the outside, through the secured window. The faux lamb's fur pillow is very comfortable!

ing material can be corrugated cardboard.

Exploring the Territory. Look at your home through the eyes of a very lively, curious, and adventurous kitten, or at least try to. Everything that moves or can be moved is seen by the kitten as legitimate prey to play with, and that includes small fashion and cosmetic accessories such as cotton balls. You had better not leave anything lying around that you do not want the kitten to get under its paws or in its teeth. Do you like to decorate shelves, cupboards, and mantlepieces with all sorts of pretty trinkets? What a lot of fun it is to dispatch these items with a few swinging paw swipes ....to the ground! You should at least put your delicate treasures in a safe place until your kitten reaches a calmer age of several years.

You should treat fancy curtains the same way: the invitation to climb them is simply irresistible for the little kitten, and you won't always be around to intervene with a firm "No."

The Permanent Place. Once the kitten starts adjusting to its new home, the time has come to think about where the cat accessories will ultimately be located. For instance, the feeding site is usually the kitchen, the litter box in an out-of-sight corner, and the scratching and climbing tree in the hallway—unless it is needed to distract from the upholstered furniture in the living room. And the sleeping bed? If the kitten is allowed in your bedroom, it can have its cat bed there, and a scratching post, too, because sharpening the claws after getting up in the morning is very much part of the cat's feeling-well ritual. In that case, you will also have to expect visits to you in bed. The decision is yours.

Safety in the New Home

TIPS FROM
CAT EXPERT
Brigitte Eilert-Overbeck

WINDOW AND BALCONY. Special sturdy nylon netting can make balcony and windows escape proof. It is essential that a proper safety latch be installed (building supply/hardware stores).

CAVES AND OTHER HIDING PLACES. Kittens will crawl into anything. Therefore, make dryers, washers, open fireplaces, ducts, cupboards, etc., inaccessible. Keep all household appliances with doors, as well as containers with lids, closed. Nevertheless, always make sure to check before you use washing machines and dryers.

ELECTRICITY. Rub or spray all cables with cat repellant or "Bitter Apple" (available from pet shops). When possible, tuck cables out of sight.

DANGEROUS SUBSTANCES. Always keep medications, cleaning agents, and other chemicals under lock and key. Similarly, secure all needles, threads, rubber bands, plastic bags (danger of suffocation), tinfoil, knitting threads, and everything else that could be swallowed by the kitten (buttons, marbles) and/or from which it could sustain an injury. Move all plants out of reach; too many are toxic.

Finally Home—Welcome, Little Kitten!

Now the kitten can come home! Maybe it will be brought to you by the breeder; otherwise it may be best for you to pick it up by car. When the carrier is padded with a pillow or small blanket from the "old home," the familiar smell will contribute to calming down the little passenger. At home, you need to close all windows and doors opening to the outside, and then take the kitten (still inside the carrier) into the prepared reception room. Open the box and then calmly sit down (ideally on the floor), and wait until the little kitten walks out of the box. If you have decided on the "double pack," this will take place very quickly; company gives courage! Show the little one (or ones) the sleeping basket, feeding place, and litter box. Keep using the same food and litter as was used in the nursery, at least for the first few days; too many changes in a short period can upset the digestive tract.

Building Trust

For the first few hours, your acting talents will be required; pretend that you are hardly interested in the kitten. Give the new arrival every opportunity to establish contact with you on its own terms. The less pressure there is (from you), the quicker the animal will gain trust in you. Play a little: let a cord wiggle along the carpet or roll a little ball. Usually it does not take long until the kitten also wants to play.

Soon your new tenant will also want to explore the rest of the home; make sure that it can do that at its own leisure. If you have a somewhat turbulent household, if there are other animals, and/or the kitten is still very shy, it may need the reception room for a few more days as a safe haven; otherwise you can leave the door open.

Patience has its reward: When the kitten comes to you without being coaxed to smell your hand, the largest fear has been overcome.

Right from the Start—A Dream Team

The kitten still feels it is in another world with you. Yet, its trust in you grows quickly when you observe a few simple ground rules and so show the kitten that you are familiar with the "feline guide to good behavior."

What to do

What not to do

During each encounter, talk to your kitten, even before you pet it. Contented cats never walk past each other without a greeting.

Cats love soft sounds, because loud noise means stress. Talk in a calm voice, and, if need be, adjust the radio or TV to a moderate volume, or use earphones.

Stay on the carpet. Your cat loves to play with you if you move down to the floor—cats prefer contacts at their eye level. Besides, you may also understand your new companion better, if (on occasion) you experience its perspective.

Do not look directly into the eyes of your cat. Among cats, the direct look is considered to be an unfriendly demonstration of power. Better: Interrupt direct eye contact with frequent looking away and winking.

Please, no cuddling attacks! Surprise contacts or movements coming suddenly from above will scare your kitten, because this is how predators attack. It gets similarly scared when it is being held against its will.

Never pick up your kitten by the nape of its neck—you could hurt it. Correctly lifting a kitten: one hand reaches around the chest and the other hand supports the posterior section.

Settling Down in the New Home Is Easy

Some kittens will do it rather quickly. A day after their arrival in a new home, they will roam curiously through the entire place, and note where food and water bowls and litter box are located; they will look for a favorite place to snooze and to observe the activities around them. Offers to play with their new owner are eagerly accepted, and eventually the kitten ends up on his or her owner's lap, purring and kneading with its paws. Kittens respond uninhibitedly to two- or four-legged family members. Most kittens like that are of pedigree breeds obtained from breeders who make special efforts with their animals during the formative period (see pages 16–19) or people who have spent quality time with their random-bred kittens to prepare them for new homes. Nevertheless, most kittens need a while longer to adjust to new impressions and to adapt to unfamiliar odors and sounds before settling down.

Nevertheless, you and your family can do a lot to make this adjustment easier for the little kitten:

› Let the new family member get used to you gradually. Stay in its proximity but without physically handling it, and frequently offer food by hand.

› Arrange for a regular daily cycle, which includes punctual meals. This gives structure to the course of a day and provides the kitten with a feeling of security.

› The more peaceful your home is, the faster the kitten gains confidence. It will see to it in due course that life gets hectic in the new home.

› Ideally, there should not be any traumatic events that might interfere with daily routines! Do not contemplate any major renovations or furniture repositioning over the next few months—your kitten must already endure sufficient changes.

› For that same reason you should also keep the kitten's newly found and accepted places for the basic accessories. Generally, you will have to show the kitten only once where everything is.

› In the event that things are not yet working out 100% with the use of the litter box, place the kitten—early in the morning and again late at night, as well as after every meal—directly into the clean box.

The kitten must absorb many new impressions before it feels totally at home in the new surroundings.

Establishing Family Ties

You should also include the other family members in this settling-in period. That will make it easier for the kitten to establish proper family ties. Occasionally, have the kitten given its food by some of the other members of the family, so that the animal does not consider you as the (exclusive) provider of food.

Cats and Children. Right from the beginning, instruct your children on the gentle and considerate handling of the new family addition. Show your child what the kitten likes, what games it enjoys, and how it likes to be touched and stroked. Explain the cat language to the child (see Behavior Explained). Convey to all family members that the kitten should be left in peace during feeding, after the meal, while sleeping, and when it is grooming itself—in fact, generally when the kitten is not in a playful or cuddling mood. Beyond that, under no circumstances leave kittens and cats alone with babies. Cats may seek out the warmth of the baby and curl up to nap on the chest of the child, which can cause breathing difficulty. It's not true that cats suck the breath of infants. That's merely a myth.

A Name for the Kitten

According to an old saying, well-behaved children have many names; certainly, so has your kitten. Nevertheless, restrict yourself to a single name to call the animal; otherwise, there will be confusion. Always address the kitten by its name while playing, cuddling, and feeding it—but never when you are loudly angry, when you are forbidding something, or when you are simply upset. Give a reward when the kitten comes in response to its name being called. This way the kitten relates its name with something pleasurable and is eager to respond to it. Of course, the name must sound pleasant. Words made up of three syllables can sound a bit like a command, and should thus be avoided. More "homey" or familiar to a kitten's ears are words with a sound like "murr"'(as in Morris or Morley), but also names with the vowels "i" and "u" are generally received well (e.g., Susie, Lilly, Minnie, Louis or—suitable for a passionate head rubbing—Zizou).

Building Golden Bridges

TIPS FROM
CAT EXPERT
Brigitte Eilert-Overbeck

Children love rituals—the bedtime story, for instance, or visiting the parents' bed for a cuddle. Such reliable, repetitive joys make for a homey feeling and strengthen trust. The same applies to kittens. Therefore, you should plan cat highlights into each day, such as:

EARLY IN THE MORNING, an extensive friendly greeting may be combined with some treat (which should be included in the calculation for the daily ration). The pleasant sound of your voice is more important than the food.

BEFORE GOING TO BED, a similarly affectionate "good night," as soon as the kitten permits this, while cuddling it. This is particularly important if your bedroom is not accessible to the kitten.

IN BETWEEN, do some fur brushing with a nice soft brush, as soon as the kitten can be handled.

KITTEN AND CAT. Initially the kitten remains in a separate room. This way both become gradually familiarized with the odor and sound of the other. Before the first encounter, rub both of them with a piece of clothing (T-shirt, sweatshirt) that you've worn so it carries your odor. This creates a kinship or family odor. Treat your "Number 1" as attentively as always; it will notice if you don't and resent the kitten for taking attention away from it. Moreover, for the kitten it is easier to adapt and to respect the established rights of the large one.

KITTEN AND DOG. While cats normally approach anyone or anything cautiously, a dog heads straight towards the object. Moreover, both have different body language; however, they can get along well as long as you mediate. Before the first encounter, both should be made familiar with the odor of the other. Rub them with towels and place the towels near the respective feeding sites. This way the odor takes on a positive meaning for both.

KITTEN AND PREY ANIMALS. A friendship can exist between cats and potential prey animals, such as parrots and rabbits; however, they must never get that close unless the human is present and provides protection, if need be.

Getting to Know the Other Animals in the House

If you act as an intermediary and familiarize the kitten gradually and patiently with an older cat or dog, it can be the beginning of a beautiful friendship, but caution is advised with other household pets, especially hunting dogs that may see a kitten as prey.

Kitten and Cat

First, accommodate your new kitten in a different separate room. Let the older cat inspect the reception room while the kitten is closed in another room or exploring the rest of the home. Give the older cat some food there, which it will appreciate. This then combines a pleasant experience with the odor of the new arrival. Prior to the first meeting between the two, rub both cats with an old, worn T-shirt. This gives both animals the same kinship or family odor, which helps them relate to each other. Give a lot of praise to the first cat, if it remains neutral or friendly toward the new one. Then, give food to both of them in feeding bowls opposite each other—each animal has its own! You may have to repeat this procedure several times, until both of them accept each other.

Kitten and Dog

 Keep both animals initially separate. Let the kitten inspect the entire home including the dog bed, while your dog smells around in the kitten's reception room. If the dog does not go berserk, the next step follows: equip yourself with doggy treats, put the dog on a leash, and open the door to the kitten's room. Concentrate only on the dog and give him a treat if he ignores the kitten. Introduce dog and kitten to each other with friendly, encouraging talk. Do not force the issue; if the kitten wants to flee back into its own room, do not pet it during the encounter. Feed both of them at separate sites, as soon as they appear to tolerate the presence of the other in a reasonably relaxed manner. Intervene immediately if the dog wants to attack the kitten, but praise it abundantly if it approaches the new family member gently.

Kitten and Rabbit

Large rabbits and gentle cats can become accustomed to each other; however, the first encounter between the two should be separated within the confines of a protective environment. Convey to the kitten that even playful hunting attempts will not be tolerated. Odor transfer (rubbing both animals with a worn T-shirt of yours) contributes to a relaxed encounter between kitten and rabbit. Nevertheless, monitor both animals closely when they approach each other without barriers. Always keep in mind that both animals have different social behavior. Rabbits are gentle with their own kind, but cats can get a bit rough in the heat of the game. That in turn would be considered an enemy attack by the rabbit. It is better to avoid such a situation.

A Healthy and Happy Kitten

When our four-legged friend is doing well, we are pleased....
who can say otherwise? We can contribute a lot to our kitten's
ongoing health and happiness, so that the animal will give us
pleasure for many years to come.

Off to a Beautiful Long Life!

Health is a precious gift that needs to be carefully nurtured among cats. It does not require great effort and you already have the most important prerequisite: love and affection! After all, affectionate touches are equally as important for kittens as they are for human children. Studies have shown that stroking and touching enhance the immune system in animals. So, keep on petting!

The second prerequisite is attention. Check regularly to see whether the kitten's eyes are clear, whether it grooms itself on a regular basis, and that its coat is shiny. You need to make sure that its appetite is good and that its digestion is normal; whether the kitten is as happy, adventurous, and curious as before—all that is indicative of good health.

A contributing factor to all that is a balanced diet (see pages 38–39). Properly nourished kittens are in top condition, a prerequisite for healthy, contented cats that have an efficient properly working internal system, strong muscles, and a stable skeletal structure.

Proper Care and Prevention

Proper care and a clean and tidy environment (see pages 40–41) are yet other keys to the good health of your new little tenant. Even though your kitten is not going to be overjoyed to visit the veterinary office, support from a competent veterinarian is essential (see page 42 onward). With his or her help you can make certain that infection does not become a danger to your little kitten, that parasites do not torment it, or that conditions grow into catastrophes; so that one day in the future, the healthy kitten under your care will become an equally healthy and happy cat senior.

A Healthy Diet Right from the Start

Small cats evolved to hunt small animals, and so they are metabolic carnivores—they can't survive without meat. However, such prey also contains other items that are eaten simultaneously: fur, skin, and bones, as well as the contents of the prey's gastrointestinal tract, which consists of pre-digested plants, mainly cereal grains. All that makes a cat's prey a so-called *whole food* item, which provides all the essential nutrients and is a well-balanced proportion of animal proteins and fats, and relatively few carbohydrates, vitamins, minerals, and trace elements.

Nutritional Basis: Manufactured Foods. Suitable prey animals are (fortunately) rarely available to our domesticated pet cats. Nevertheless, our pets do not have to go without a suitable whole food diet: highly nutritional prepared (ready-to-use) foods also contain all essential nutrients in suitably balanced proportions. For kittens during their first year of life, specially developed kitten food is the best choice, because it is tailored to meet their elevated protein and energy requirements. At that stage, kittens need a lot of protein, especially the essential amino acid *taurine* (aminoethionic acid) for optimal development of muscle, vision, and brain. Carbohydrates and animal fats provide the required energy source. These dietary components are also required by cats for synthesizing essential amino acids. Vitamins, minerals, and trace elements are important for strong teeth and bones, healthy skin, attractive coat, and an efficient immune system. Finally, the food also contains roughage (fiber) required for healthy digestion.

The Correct Drink. A drink of milk for the kitten? Please don't, water is better! Many cats will get diarrhea from lactose; exception: *"cat milk"* with reduced lactose content, but this is more of a food item than a drink, given to motherless kittens.

Healthy nibbles: occasionally a little dab of yogurt or cottage cheese may even be licked directly off your finger.

In spite of a dislike for water: free-roaming cats like to drink from the edge of a stream or pond in a manner much like their wild relatives.

On the Subject of Dry Food

DRY FOOD is simple, practical, nutritional, and good for the teeth, but is not suitable for many kittens. Moisture has been largely removed from such food. To avoid kidney problems, the moisture deficit must be compensated for with water.

EASIER SAID THAN DONE. By nature, cats drink only sparingly, so you should give the largest amount of the daily food ration in the form of moist, prepared (canned) food, and use dry food only as a supplement. Have several water bowls available, and read the instructions on the dry food pack. With dry and wet food brands, the ingredients will be listed by order of weight, with the most plentiful as the first ingredient. The other ingredients are listed in descending order.

Little Extras. An occasional offering of butter from the tip of a spoon, or some (boiled) egg yolk scrambled over the food, will provide valuable proteins, fats, and vitamins. From time to time, a small portion of yogurt or cottage cheese is beneficial for the intestinal flora and—unlike milk—it is well tolerated by the kitten. The pet supply store offers all sorts of treats for cats. They are useful as rewards, but should be used sparingly, because in the long term they are fattening.

Dietary Timetable for a Kitten

Live-wire kittens will burn up calorie-rich foods without any problem. Nevertheless, do not get into the habit of over-feeding, because early "kitten sins" tend to catch up with adult cats after 18 months to two years, manifesting themselves as excess weight.

› Up to an age of three months (17–35 oz. body weight), $\frac{1}{2}$ lb. of canned food (wet kitten formula) per day, spread out over four to five portions, is sufficient, with an additional 1–1.5 oz of dry kitten food freely available.

› At four to five months of age (17 oz–3 lbs. body weight), it can handle $\frac{1}{2}$–$\frac{3}{4}$ lb. canned food (wet kitten formula), spread out over three to four portions, with an additional 1.5–2 oz of dry kitten food.

› By six to 11 months (3 – 6$\frac{1}{2}$ lbs.), the kitten will eat $\frac{2}{3}$–$\frac{3}{4}$ lbs. of canned food, distributed over two to three meals, as well as 2–2.5 oz dry kitten food.

› From an age of 12 months on (6.5–10 lbs.), your cat should get 8–13 oz. canned food (wet, adult formula) per day, distributed over two meals. In addition, there should be 2.5–3 oz. of dry adult cat food, freely accessible.

All amounts listed are averages and vary somewhat depending on the activity and size of the cat and the quality of the food.

A Properly Looked-after Cat Is a Healthy Cat

Wild cats will easily spend three hours per day grooming themselves. This is not out of vanity; it is the hunter's way to remove revealing odors from larger preditors, maintain its coat so that it won't get hung up anywhere, look after its weapons (claws), and keep in shape. The grooming program is essential for its survival and is done instinctively, particularly after a meal, to remove the smell of blood and other prey odors.

Your kitten also likes to groom itself. Your support in this is not only a welcome source of attention, but a way to keep an eye on the kitten's health and notice when something is amiss.

Care of the Coat. Acquaint your kitten early with a comb and brush. Loose hairs that have been brushed off can no longer be swallowed during grooming, thus avoiding the formation of trouble-

Grooming is fun! A kitten will groom itself for about 3½ hours a day . . . just like adult cats.

some hairballs. Also, loose hairs do not end up on clothes, upholstered armchairs, or carpets.

> Shorthair kittens should be combed once or twice a week (more frequently during molting in spring and fall), gently from head to tail; do not forget the abdominal region, the axillary areas behind the front and hind limbs, and the genital area. After brushing, loose hairs should be removed. Always comb the right way and use a comb with flexible teeth; it removes more fur, without unduly pulling hair.

> For breeds with super-short hair, merely wipe down the coat with a damp chamois (leather) cloth.

> For longhaired cats, turn the entire grooming procedure into a daily ritual. You can undo some of the smaller knots with a gentle touch before they become matted. Add an ample amount of petting, and at the end give a treat as a bonus.

Eyes and Ears. Crusts or tears in the corners of the eyes can be removed with a damp tissue or a wet cleaning cloth from the pet supply store. Also clean out the external ear (*pinna*) occasionally. The presence of dirt, unpleasant odors, and frequent head shaking are indicative of ear mites. See a vet for all your cats; mites are contagious.

Teeth. Dental plaque can be recognized by discoloration and mouth odor. As a preventative measure, the teeth should be brushed with a special brush (if your cat lets you) in conjunction with feeding a type of dry food. During immunization appointments, have the veterinarian examine the cat's teeth and remove any dental deposits (scale).

Claws. Removing dead nail from the claws by scratching is the best kind of maintenance! Similarly, the cats remove dead claw sheaths with their

Encrusted material and debris accumulated in the corners of the eyes can be removed with a soft, damp cloth.

Very well-behaved cats will permit having their teeth brushed, using a special toothbrush and fish-flavored toothpaste.

teeth on occasion. Cutting the claws manually is necessary about every two to three weeks. Your veterinarian will show you how this is done.

Clean Environment

Cats also appreciate cleanliness in their living space. Your kitten will be contented if:

> Every meal is served in a clean feeding bowl with no leftover bits lying around. Wash and refill the water bowl each day.

> The cover of its sleeping bed is changed frequently—cats like to lay on newly washed laundry.

> Its litter box is clean. Add a two-inch layer of scoopable litter; remove fecal matter as soon as possible and lumps of urine daily. Wash it out with hot water and scrub it with a brush each week or every other week, depending on the size and number of cats in the household.

> Parasites are kept away (see page 44). When combing the kitten with a flea comb, watch for "tiny dark passengers" and remove ticks with tick

removal tools (wear gloves and wash your hands afterwards). If the cat carries fleas, your entire home will need to be treated: all resting places and curtains up to 3½ feet off the floor should be sprayed with a cat-safe flea product; covers, blankets, and pillows must be washed frequently. See your veterinarian for suggestions on flea control— breakthroughs have been made, like products with fipronil that only need to be applied once a month.

Check for Fleas

Comb the kitten using a flea comb over a light-colored floor or table area and occasionally work against the grain. If any small remnants are left behind in the comb or if black "crumbs" fall off the coat, rub them with wet fingers. If doing that leaves blood-red traces, they come from flea feces. Anti-flea substances may be obtained from pet supply stores or your veterinarian.

Off to the Veterinarian? No Problem!

What happens when your cat has to be taken to the vet? Every owner knows what a cat or kitten will do before the animal is finally inside the transport box; it will hide, flee, and fight with extended claws. **Relaxed in the Box.** Therefore, it is better to get your kitten accustomed to the transport box well before you have to take the animal to a veterinarian. Place a blanket or pillow inside, place the container on the floor with the door open—and simply walk away. Sooner or later the little cave explorer will be inside. Let the kitten reach for its toys through the slots on the box and give a lot of praise. Close the door briefly, give more praise, and offer the kitten a treat through the mesh. Open the door again and walk away to do something else. Repeat that routine frequently and carry the box briefly with the kitten inside. Give a reward if the kitten appears to be unafraid inside the box, and ignore it briefly when it leaves the transport box. With a lot of praise and some treats, many kittens can be trained to enter the box on request.

Preventive Medicine and Control

Even a very healthy cat should be taken to a vet at least once a year—for a general examination, possibly also for some preventative worming and immunizations (see Immunization Schedule). Take advice from your veterinarian about what immunizations cover your kitten's needs.

Feline Parvovirus (FPV). Parvovirus is extremely resilient and a danger even to those cats without contact with other cats. Only proper immunization can offer adequate protection. This is a MUST!

"Cat Flu." Is transmitted via Herpes and Caliciviruses, which cause severe respiratory ailments. Immunization is absolutely essential!

Feline Leukemia Virus: The feline leukemia virus (FelV) is transferred by means of droplet infection

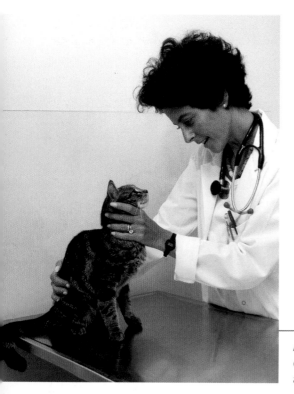

A kitten's health with a gentle touch: with such a compassionate handler, every visit to the veterinarian is a relaxed affair.

from one cat to another, and can cause fatal FelV. Kittens that have contact with other cats must be immunized.

FiP. The causative agents of "feline infectious peritonitis" are Corona viruses, which are transmitted from animal to animal. This often terminal disease causes fluid accumulations in the abdominal cavity, respiratory ailments, and severe systemic damage. The kitten must have tested negative prior to immunization.

Chlamydia. An infection by Chlamydia leads to severe conjunctivitis. This is a threat principally for cats that live in close association with other cats.

Rabies. This fatal virus infection is transferred through the saliva of infected animals (e.g., skunks, raccoons). An immunization is essential for free-roaming cats; indoor cats taken out of the country must also be immunized against rabies.

Find Your Lost Kitten

Sadly, the majority of cats that are lost will never be returned to their owner. Your kitten has a much better chance, however, if it is microchipped—a tiny rice-shaped device is inserted under the skin and can be read with a special scanner. Inserting the chip is painless and, unlike a tattoo, it does not require an anesthetic. Such identification is not only recommended if your kitten is to travel with you; it is essential that a free-roaming kitten is microchipped and then registered at an appropriate pet registry (see page 62). The chances of finding a lost cat are much greater if the animal carries a microchip and has been registered.

Immunization Plan for Your Kitten

IMMUNIZATION	BASIC SERIES			BOOSTER
	1st immun. at an age of	Repeat immun. at an age of	Final immun. at an age of	
FELINE PARVOVIRUS (FPV)	8 weeks	12 & 16 weeks	15 months	every 3 years*
CAT FLU	8 weeks	12 & 16 weeks	15 months	every 3 years*
(FEL-V)	9–10 weeks	12–14 weeks	15 months	annually
FIP	16 weeks	20 weeks	15 months	annually
RABIES	12 weeks	16 weeks	16 months	every 1–3 years*
CHLAMYDIA	8–9 weeks	11–13 weeks	15 months	every 3 years

*depending on vaccine used

Note: For adult animals with minimal risks of infection (e.g., indoor cats without contact with other cats), the interval between booster immunizations for Feline Parvovirus, Cat Flu, and FeLV can be longer. Discuss this with your veterinarian. Have your cat immunized early in case you plan to travel or attend exhibitions and shows. Remember: protection builds up gradually.

A Sick Kitten—What to Do?

If, in spite of all precautions, your kitten gets sick, an effective medication is usually quickly available. **Parasites—A Real Pest.** For abdominal pain, vomiting, and diarrhea, a worm infestation is often the cause. Usually these are roundworms (*Ascaris*), but it can also be a tapeworm. The kitten becomes infested by eating mice, raw fish, or meat or when it bites on and swallows an infested flea. Get worming medication (vermicide) from your veteri-

narian, clean the cat box with a disinfectant tolerated by cats (pet supply store), and maintain meticulous hygiene—these worms can also infect humans. Regular worming (3–4 times a year for free-roaming cats, once or twice annually for indoor cats) usually provides sufficient protection. Excessive scratching is a sign of skin parasites, usually fleas (see pages 40–41). These torment cats and also transmit tapeworms and other parasites, and will also bite humans. Cats that are badly infested with fleas may have to be bathed, but often flea drops (drops placed on the neck) or other substances are sufficient. Consult your veterinarian! Many cats cannot tolerate flea collars.

Dangerous Diseases

Cats rarely infect humans with their diseases, but there are exceptions.

Toxoplasmosis. Cats get this by eating raw, uncooked meat (e.g., scraps or prey). The pathogens are excreted via feces, which can be dangerous for pregnant women by damaging the fetus. About 40 percent of women and their progeny are safe due to an earlier, undetected infection. A toxoplasmosis test by your doctor can tell. Prevention: do not feed uncooked meats, remove feces quickly (pathogens become active after 48 hours), and clean the cat box using rubber gloves.

Ringworm. Broken hairs, bare spots along the

Anyone who looks that bright-eyed and curious to the world is in the best of health, but protection against parasites is still essential.

coat, and scaly patches, inflammations, and itching indicate a contagious fungus infection. Apart from medication, this also requires precautionary measures: everything in contact with the kitten must be disinfected. Any contact with its skin or coat is prohibited without gloves!

Rabies. If a human has been bitten by a rabid animal, immediate shots will save him or her. Once symptoms appear, there is no help for the animal, but immunization affords effective protection!

On the Way to Recovery—Nursing Care

When your kitten is not feeling well, it will tend to withdraw. Respect its need for rest and monitor its behavior inconspicuously. Should the little patient have an infection and there are also other animals in the home, it must be isolated immediately.

> Using pillows, provide padding into a low box (keep changing pillow covers!) and place it in the "sick ward" in a quiet, draft-free corner.

> Place food and water close by and a separate cat box at a distance, but in the same room.

> Your voice is a healing factor! Talk in a calm and friendly voice, especially when handling.

> Medication is most readily taken when hidden inside a treat. If that does not work, have your veterinarian show you how to administer it.

> The animal's temperature is most easily taken by two people: one holds on to the shoulders and front paws of the kitten, and the other inserts the lubricated thermometer into the anus. The normal temperature is 100.4–102.2 degrees Fahrenheit.

> In an emergency, immediately call for professional help (veterinarian, emergency vet services). Remain calm to pacify the frightened kitten.

What Makes a Good Veterinarian

TIPS FROM
CAT EXPERT
Brigitte Eilert-Overbeck

You will get lots of advice from other cat fanciers, breeding associations, animal welfare groups, and the Internet when you are looking for a good, reliable veterinarian for your kitten. In the end, however, it is your personal impression that will decide. You will need to find the partner for your cat's life to be pleasant and engaging, even though your kitten is—most likely—not going to share that feeling. When visiting your vet's office, look for the following points:

THE OFFICE conveys a well-organized impression. The receptionist is friendly and attentive.

THE VETERINARIAN talks not only to you but also to your kitten.

THE VETERINARIAN AND ASSISTANTS know the correct handling of the animal and barely need to apply any force.

THE VETERINARIAN TAKES HIS OR HER TIME to answer your questions, explains what is being done; and then tells you exactly how you can best support the treatment of your kitten.

The Most Important Diseases and Their Treatments

DISEASE/SYMPTOMS	WHAT TO DO?	WHEN YOU MUST GO AND SEE THE VET?
LOSS OF APPETITE	Try warming up the food	After two days at the latest
EYE REMAINS CLOSED	Likely conjunctivitis	After 24 hours at the latest
MASSIVE MOBILITY IMPAIRMENT (STAGGERING, LEGS GIVING OUT)		Immediately
CONJUNCTIVITIS, WEEPING EYE	Clean corners of the eye with cool water, avoid drafts	After two days at the latest
VOMITING, DIARRHEA	Check the food, possibly give meaty broth or tuna juice, monitor general condition	After 24 hours at the latest
VOMITING, DIARRHEA WITH BLOOD, FOAM, OR MUCUS		Immediately! Emergency!
SKIN RASH	Check for parasites	After one week at the latest
LIMPING	Monitor general condition	After two days
COUGHING	Monitor general condition	When animal coughs conspicuously often
COUGHING AND/OR SNEEZING, FEVER, RESPIRATORY DIFFICULTIES	Keep the animal warm	Immediately!
BELLY ACHE, HARD ABDOMEN	Cover the animal, and make sure the cat does not injure itself	Immediately!
PROLAPSE OF NICTITATING MEMBRANE; 3RD EYELID VISIBLE WHEN EYE IS OPEN	Monitor general condition; several causes possible	As soon as possible
SALIVATING, RUBBING MOUTH	Force mouth open with pressure exerted at corner of the mouth; if possible remove foreign object	After 24 hours at the latest
ACCIDENTAL INJURIES (I.E., HIT BY CAR OR LONG FALL)	Remove cat gently from danger zone with as little movement as possible	Immediately! Emergency!
CONSTIPATION	Avoid dry food; offer butter or oily sardine, possibly mix $1/2$ teaspoon of oil in with food	After 24 hours at the latest
CONSTIPATION (MASSIVE), VOMITING, HARD ABDOMINAL AREA		Immediately! Emergency!
BEHAVIORAL CHANGES (APATHY, AGGRESSION)		Immediately!

What Can Alternative Medicine Do for My Kitten?

In many respects, alternative healing procedures, including home medicines (herbs, compresses) can also be helpful for kittens, as long as the therapist not only has the required expertise, but also is familiar with cats. Yet, he or she must also know his or her own limitations. After all, there is no way past the veterinarian, even if it is only for the required immunizations. Apart from non-veterinary practitioners and animal therapists, some veterinarians also offer alternative therapies in addition to conventional veterinary medicine. Such therapies are to activate self-healing powers, dissolve energy blockages, and re-establish the inner equilibrium.

The Most Important Alternative Healing Methods

Homeopathy. This method does not fight diseases with antidotes but instead uses the principle of "equal heals equal." For that purpose, extremely low doses of substances are used, with the intent of stimulating the body's system to heal itself. Cats and kittens with allergies, eczemas, bronchitis, or cold symptoms and other infections apparently respond well to homeopathic medicines, which can also be effective against general weakness and loss of appetite.

Bach Flower Therapy. The energy of certain blossoms acts positively on the psyche of humans and animals. This was the assumption of the founder of this school of therapy, Dr. Edward Bach. His hypothesis was that each organic disease is accompanied by a disorder of the psyche. When the latter has been resolved, the disease symptoms will disappear. The effect of the blossom essences cannot be scientifically proven, yet many cat owners report success with this method. Of special note are the "emergency drops" (a "rescue remedy") which appear to calm down even highly agitated or distraught animals.

Acupuncture. Traditional Chinese medicine teaches that the energy flow in the body flows in particular passages, the meridians. The presence of an illness means that this flow has been impeded. At certain locations on the skin—acupuncture points—this flow can be triggered through stimulation with acupuncture needles so that energy flows again. In cats, acupuncture is used primarily for ailments afflicting locomotion apparatus or for pain reduction, but also for hematological disease and weakness of the immune system.

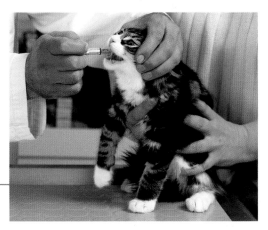

Gentle force: administering medication with a disposable syringe (no needle).

Getting Along Well Together

You love your kitten. That is already an excellent ingredient for a harmonious relationship. Yet, for both of you to live happily and satisfied, side by side, requires a little bit more: understanding and some clear, unambiguous rules.

Maintaining the Relationship . . . Made Easy

Cats do as they please, and this can lead to a conflict in the home if and when the cat's owner wants something different. After all, here are two entities squaring off who have equal rights. In other words, you may own the home—but your kitten feels that *it* owns the territory. Two bosses, and both expect that their rules apply; if both insist unyieldingly on their respective rights, trouble is virtually guaranteed. You complain loudly about scratch marks on the upholstered furniture and on wallpaper, with the result that the little kitten feels picked on. If, on the other hand, you permit everything, the little boss will become the sole ruler. Neither you nor your kitten will be happy with such an arrangement.

Consequently, there will have to be compromises. Moreover, there is some good news here: if you are willing to invest a little attention, patience, and understanding in this relationship, your kitten is quite willing to come to terms with you and accept certain rules. This is an innate response—even the wildest relatives of your kitten that share a territory negotiate the rules with each other; this may involve an occasional argument where claws and bites are used. However, once the relationship has been defined, the motto among cats is, "live and let live."

Training, Play, and Tenderness

The atmosphere can be just as relaxed in your joint territory at home, of course, without any physical altercation to resolve the guidelines of your relationship. Instead, issues can be resolved with intelligent education (see pages 50–53), understanding for the kitten's territorial needs (see pages 54–55), support by stimulating play and occupational activities (see pages 56–58), and with lots of tender affection (see page 59). This is not only good for the kitten—its purring also comforts the human soul.

Training—The Art of Making *Contracts!*

In an ideal case, your kitten had a good upbringing, is housebroken, knows how to get along with other cats in the home, and treats all members of its new family like those of its own kind. The kitten is aware it must come to terms with others in its territory. This is your opportunity! You do not achieve success by ordering the kitten around or striking it—only by "contracts" based on reciprocity.

Off-limit Areas. Your kitten wants to explore all of its new territory into the smallest corner; for safety reasons you cannot permit this without restrictions. Your contract: certain areas are excluded from territorial rights—for instance the stovetop, kitchen cupboards, drawers, and the dining table. If the kitten moves in the direction of any of these "off-limit areas," call out with a loud voice "No!" or clap your hands. If that does not stop the exploring drive, you will have to reinforce your "No." Position empty tin cans along the edges of the forbidden area, which will crash to the floor with a loud noise

If you want to minimize scratch marks on upholstered furniture, provide several attractive scratching facilities, and praise the animal warmly when it uses them.

when the animal jumps up on this prohibited area. Alternatively, cover these areas with two-sided sticky tape. You will soon be able to remove these because the kitten will have learned not to go there.

Stealing. Stealing is not an offense within cat circles. Every object the little predator can obtain through strength, agility, and speed will be considered legitimate prey. Your contract: anything that is lying or standing around unguarded in the home, you are expected to have "approved" (see pages 28–29). Your kitten may "acquire" it unless it is on a prohibited site, such as a piece of meat on a kitchen table; however, even there, such a tempting morsel should not be left in plain sight.

Begging. Why should your kitten not be allowed occasionally to sample a piece of roast beef or chicken from the dining table? Because this will teach the animal to beg. Your contract: food is given exclusively at the established feeding site, and the kitten is ignored at the human dining table. Of course, a piece of human food can be placed at the regular feeding site, but only there.

Scratching. Your little companion needs to remove dead nail from its claws, but not on furniture, carpets, or walls! Your contract: You provide attractive scratching facilities, and your kitten will scratch only there. If the animal sinks its claws into the wrong objects, an unequivocal "No" is due. Distract the animal with an offer to play and coax it to its scratching post. Heap praise on the animal if it uses the facility. You will need to do this frequently, because the kitten will instantly submit to its scratching drive wherever it is overcome by it. You need to realize, though, that your home will not remain totally without any scratch marks, no matter what you do, but you know that already. . .

Basic Training Rules

TIPS FROM
CAT EXPERT
Brigitte Eilert-Overbeck

Cats are headstrong and will always remain so. Take that into consideration when training the animal. If you do that, you will save yourself a lot of frustration and be more successful.

PROHIBITIONS should only be used sparingly, but you must enforce those few taboos with vigilance, consistency, and friendliness. Your kitten will be confused if a particular prohibition is enforced sometimes, but not on other occasions.

TRANSGRESSIONS should immediately be responded to with a strong "No" or with hand clapping. When dangerous escapades occur (e.g., jumping onto a stove), blow air in the kitten's face, equivalent to hissing "*Do not do that!*"

PENALTIES should not even be contemplated. Beating is out of the question anyway, but even loud cursing will only induce fear and is useless. Your kitten will not relate retroactive measures to previous misdeeds, and so it feels harassed without reason and therefore loses its trust in you.

DESIRED BEHAVIOR should be enforced with praise and a reward, but react quickly!

Fit for a Free Run

Are the conditions right for your kitten to roam (see page 10) in a securely fenced off outdoor territory? Before your pet can go on its first outdoor excursion, you need to make sure that it is thoroughly familiar with its new home, and it must respond to its name. After about four weeks, the time is usually right for such an adventure. Go to the outside enclosure with the kitten and let it walk around for a while; maintain voice and sight contact at all times, and ask the animal to come inside again after about 30 minutes or so. Upon safe return inside you should give your pet a treat as a reward. During the following days, you can extend the time spent outdoors. Once the kitten returns reliably in response to your call, you can allow the animal to go to its enclosure on its own. If you can provide a cat door from the enclosure to the house, all the

better! Do not forget the treat when the kitten returns. Shaking the treat container has proven to be an effective enhancement of the return call. A cat that is permitted to go outdoors must be able to return indoors at any time it desires, e.g., through a cat door or flap, one you can lock when needed. Keep in mind that some diseases and many parasites can infect your cat even in the enclosure, unless it is completely made of plastic, wood, or drywall, which defeats the purpose of an outdoor enclosure.

Leash Training

Without an outdoor run, enclosure, or a balcony, you can then take your kitten outside only on a leash. Training the kitten to walk on a leash also comes in handy when you are traveling, visiting your veterinarian, or when moving.

> Get an ordinary kitten collar and then let the kitten play with it for a while.

> Then simply put the collar on the kitten, but take it off again after five minutes. Repeat this several times. Praise the kitten if it lets you do it, but do not force the issue if it resists; some kittens simply will not do it. Well, what then?

> If the collar training does not work, get a chest harness (one specifically for cats) and a leash. The harness is safer and ultimately more comfortable. A neck collar can get caught on objects and can strangle your cat. Let the kitten play with the harness for a while until you put it on for the first time for about five minutes.

> After a few repeats of this procedure (stop when the kitten does not want to do it anymore), clip the

"I'm not doing anything!" With the innocent face of a youngster, *spiderman* can expect a severe scolding.

leash onto the harness, take it in one hand and hold a treat in the other, coaxing the animal to move forward. With every step, you give praise, and finally the kitten gets a treat.

Practice this patiently and offer much praise; never leave the kitten unattended when on a leash.

Some Extra Coaching

If there are gaps in a kitten's early education, subsequent training may not be as easy. For instance, small strays need a little longer until they trust their new owner and accept him or her as a "contract partner." Some may never learn things like retracting their claws when playing, or not to become frightened when they hear certain sounds—even if it is only the toaster popping. Other things they may learn with a bit more effort, such as not to use plant dishes as a cat box, or that claws are allowed only to be sharpened on specific objects.

With patience and positive reinforcement, you will also be able to overcome these hurdles. Praise the little fellow as soon as it shows the desired behavior, for example: your kitten uses its litter box properly or sinks its claws into the scratching facility provided. Click your tongue in appreciation and subsequently offer it a treat.

It is important that you click your tongue exactly at the moment when the action takes place, so that your kitten understands the praise and relates it to the action. This method of *"praise immediately, reward follows soon thereafter"* is like the clicker training used successfully with dogs; it also works with kittens and cats.

Yet, positive reinforcement alone is not enough. Kittens can hang on persistently to their old bad habits. Wherever a terse "No" or hand clapping don't work, other inhibiting stimuli may have the appropriate effect. Here, too, it is imperative to act

Even a pigheaded kitten, like this blue British Shorthair, can be trained with love, patience, and persistence.

instantly! Example: For the tenth time, your kitten is heading for the armrest on your sofa to sharpen its claws there. A well-aimed shot of plain water from a plastic spray bottle will discourage the misdeed. "Shoot" from a hiding place, so that the kitten does not associate the squirt with you, but instead the action of the claws on the wrong object. The kitten must not know where the shooter is. After a few repeats, the kitten will have learned its lesson.

Composure Is the Key

Whatever you do as a cat trainer, approach it in a relaxed manner. Many bad habits, such as an accident away from the litter box, can be due to the stress from a changed environment (which can have far-reaching effects on a kitten's digestive process) or an excess of energy such as the popular event of "curtain climbing" (see pages 28–29). These types of problems can be resolved within a few weeks while having a lot of fun (see pages 56–57).

Dream Territory for an Indoor Cat

These cats or kittens must be contented with a life within your walls. Your apartment or house provides the little co-owner with adequate territory. Usually this does not present a problem—unless you have too many cats for the size of your home. Your kitten likes to be comfortable and have things to lay and perch upon.

Life "Under Cover." The kitten likes recesses, curtains, plush sofa and bed covers, tablecloths that hang down to the floor—in short, everything that provides cover. These preferences have been inherited from wild ancestors in the jungles and savannahs of Africa. Just like them, our indoor cat also likes to sneak along hidden trails. Plant containers cleverly arranged can create such a jungle trail but, of course, the plants in them must be non-toxic,

Sweet dreams high up on bookshelves: cats and literature have always been a good combination.

such as bamboo, umbrella plants, spider plants, thyme, and catnip.

Looking Down on It. If possible, the kitten's ceiling-high scratch and climbing tree, with a little nook to hide in and a viewing platform, should not remain the only climbing facility available to your pet. Looking for views from the top is also one of the genetically-inherited preferences of the kitten. Therefore, you can let the animal jump safely onto wardrobes, cupboards, and shelves; you should also clear a little space on the windowsill, so that the kitten can look through the window and enjoy the panoramic view. Maybe you can also sacrifice one or two sections along the top of a set of high-rise shelves, which you can make accessible via climbing aids such as thick ropes. Even an alcove can be turned into a very attractive cat playground with suspended ceiling lofts or long shelving along the walls, at a level just above door height (your kitten also appreciates straight areas where balls can be rolled along with great ease). In case furniture in the vicinity is insufficient as jumping-off points or intermediate landing places, provide alternative access: a branch secured to the wall, a piece of lumber with cross rungs, a do-it-yourself step structure, ladder, or thick ropes.

It Must Be the Entire Home. Your kitten will want to roam throughout the entire home, be it an apartment or a house. A forbidden room (e.g., the bedroom) will be accepted, but only as a territorial border. Yet, this does not exclude the occasional venture into such an off-limits space, under the motto *"Laws are made to be broken."* It would be nice (especially for your furniture) if there were also

Dream home: comfortable for two-legged creatures and a stimulating territory for an indoor cat, with recesses, "caves," viewing platforms, climbing opportunities, cat-compatible plants, and a secure balcony as an open-air resort.

several permanently installed claw-scratching facilities; for instance, sisal mats attached to the wall or on the floor to protect the carpet.

Outdoor Enclosure: The Balcony

A kitten's "dream territory" also includes a balcony if possible. Here your kitten can enjoy fresh air and experience seasonal temperature and climate changes, sunbathe, or dream about snowflakes. Such an open-air enclosure must be secured with a cat protection net (pet supply store or hardware store). Are you more or less prepared to surrender the entire balcony to your kitten or cat? In that case, attach the net so that it forms an enclosed veranda. Equipped with a climbing tree, cat "nook" and viewing platforms, it becomes an open-air resort for your pet. Moreover, if there is enough space left for a table and some folding chairs, you might be allowed to even join your pet.

Fitness Training—Fun for Cat and Man

Kittens must play—not only to have fun, but also in order to remain fit. For an indoor cat, play is even more important as a substitute for hunting and as physical training: it is the best way for the kitten to maintain its level of intelligence, joy of life, and mobility well into an advanced age. If you have two kittens you will hardly have to give any thought to the sporting component of their play activities; the kittens will chase each other, fall over each other, and engage in simulated fights—all a lot of exercise and fun! Nevertheless, do not be fooled—no kitten likes to do without play sessions with humans.

Fitness Center: Climbing Tree. It is understood that your kitten is allowed to play anywhere; however, it will find its scratch and climbing tree even more tempting—and your pet is more likely to use its claws on it—if you turn the tree into a fitness center. To do that, you do not need to be a skilled handyman; what it requires is cat psychology. Therefore, it is best to start the daily play rounds at the climbing tree. Wiggle a soft cord up the trunk of the tree; let your kitten follow a cloth mouse pulled up by a string, or wiggle a feather toy; or the light beam from a cat-safe laser beam toy. Don't point directly at the cat's eyes!. Occasionally hang new toys in the tree, such as little balls or tassels suspended with very short cords. The important point here is that the kitten understands: the tree is a play and fun center. You should also deposit the "treasure chest" there; it contains all those items the kitten is currently not playing with.

Games for Two. Roll a few soft foam rubber balls and admire the kitten's ability to "kick" them. Very popular are balls with rattling internal objects. Some love to wobble not-quite-spherical objects around the floor because of their irregular rolling pattern: walnuts, empty thread spools, a plastic Easter egg.....throw a little rubber ball against the wall and you find that the little athlete jumps at the balls and will get nearly every one. The kitten will catch small, lightweight little balls, catnip toys, scrunched-up paper balls or bottle corks while in

Even when fully grown, the cat will be able to stand up against such a solidly built scratching post.

HIGH-WIRE ARTIST. It does not always need to be boards and ladders – even a thick rope will be an invitation to your kitten to climb, but not only that. After all, cats are balancing artists that can turn circus artists green with envy. Under a circus tent, safety nets provide security, but you do not need to worry about that; however, a rope for your kitten must not be strung above a hard floor. In the event the animal accidentally falls, it is better to land on something soft on the climbing tree or on some padded areas around it.

TUNNEL HAPPINESS. Getting fit on the scratching and climbing tree works well, but this is by no means the only sporting activity. Your kitten, as a passionate cave explorer, will enjoy playing in a toy tunnel. It is amazing what can be done with something like that: racing through it, playing hide-and-seek, reaching through the tunnel for your hand, rolling around with the tunnel or—when it has more self-confidence—being rolled around in it.

FOR THOSE GOING UP. Small mountain climbers have high objectives. With proper climbing aids, all opportunities are wide open. The space gained in this manner turns a small home into a large territory.

Angling, scratching, and catching game all in one: when it is alone, the kitten can have a lot of fun with a "Play'n'Scratch" toy.

"Catch the feather duster"—you can bring a lot of joy to your kitten, with games like this or similar ones.

flight and may even retrieve them. And what about a game of hide-and-seek? Place a sturdy paper bag (do not use plastic bags due to the danger of suffocation) on the floor and possibly add some dried catnip. Of course, the inquisitive kitten will crawl into the bag and you have to "look" for it, while it rolls around inside the bag and tries to reach for you through the sides of the bag.

Solitary Games. Of course, your kitten can also at times amuse itself. Place a box with rustling tissue paper on the floor, and the kitten will immediately dive in with pleasure. Alternately, offer a shoebox with holes where you have hidden a few treats or a little toy: a wonderful fishing game! Moreover, when you occasionally give the kitten an empty paper towel or toilet paper roll, the animal will be thrilled.

Rules of the Game. The fun will remain unspoiled, provided you

> Offer, but do not pressure.

> Stop when the kitten has lost interest or shows the first threat of defense.

> Let your game partner catch the "prey" on the third attempt, at the latest.

Toys Are Not a Waste of Time

A kitten will play with everything that comes under its paws, but it also enjoys regular cat toys. The pet supply store carries a wide selection.

> Classical items are mice made of sisal, faux fur, or fabric. Some contain rattling material. Some toys emit realistic sounds from a built-in microchip. Toy mice make excellent "prey," but you must make sure that they are safe to play with; sewn-on plastic eyes or button noses can be bitten off and swallowed by your kitten. You will need to remove these items before giving these toys to your kitten.

> Little sacks or socks filled with catnip will create harmless intoxication in some cats, while others remain only moderately affected. Remember: sewn-on bells or other small ornaments must first be removed!

› Your kitten likes ball games of all kinds. Most preferred are little balls with a diameter of 1 to 2 inches; these will roll nicely, are easy to move, and can also be carried as "prey" in the mouth, especially when they are nice and soft.

› Interactive toys, such as a fishing rod or plastic stick with "fishing line" and soft "prey" or feathers (with a rod, cord, and colorful feathers) are ideal for a kitten's fitness training—provided you are also playing. However, never let your kitten play with strings and sticks and the like alone—there are inherent accident dangers!

› Solitary games enhance intelligence and mobility, such as "Play'n'Scratch," a combination fishing, scratching, and catching game, or a flat wooden box with holes on top and the sides and balls that need to be "fished" out. Your kitten can have fun with that for hours; yet, it still prefers to play with you—several times a day for 10 to 15 minutes each.

Time for Affection

Kittens have virtually boundless energy. If they could only pass some of that on to us stressed-out, two-legged creatures! Don't worry—they can! Kittens not only like to play, eat, and sleep—somewhere along the line is also time to cuddle. Of course, it has to be out of its own motivation. Tempting the kitten with a soft voice is permitted, but actually reaching for it is okay only if the kitten has clearly signaled its consent and likes to be picked up. Once the little kitten sits gently purring on your lap, you feel quickly how your own empty energy reservoirs are filled again. Close your eyes and absorb the purring vibrations. This feels good—just like a gentle miniature massage. Moreover, in no time you feel refreshed, brighter, and better all around. And your little kitten? It enjoys

the petting and feels contented just like a baby with its mother. By the way, two kittens will readily play with each other and eat at the same time, but they will cuddle up with their owner only one at a time. Consequently, you will need to give each kitten its very own snuggle-time and do not even attempt to pet both of them at the same time—that creates jealousy and leads to unnecessary arguments.

How much your kitten enjoys these cuddle sessions, of course, also depends on how it is being stroked. The most important point here is that it must be done with real feeling. You would not like purely mechanical stroking. Let your hands, with very light pressure and flowing movements, glide over the back, flanks, and chest area. Behind the ears, under the chin, along the cheeks, neck, and back of the head, cats like to be gently scratched using your fingers. Cats usually do not like to be touched on the abdomen, paws, and tails, and so you had better leave those areas alone.

Feel-good Massage

Periodically some cats appreciate a feel-good massage; however, you should only stroke with very light pressure. Start behind the ears and continue all the way down to the root of the tail. You have to find out for yourself whether your kitten prefers slow stroking, circular motions, or rhythmic kneading. Note: At the slightest sign of any displeasure, this activity must stop.

Cat Associations

> American Association of Cat Enthusiasts (AACE)
P.O. Box 213
Pine Brook, NJ 07058
(973) 335-6717
www.aaceinc.org
> American Cat Fanciers Association (ACFA)
P.O. Box 203
Point Lookout, MO 65726
(417) 334-5430
www.acfacat.com
> Canadian Cat Association (CCA)
220 Advance Blvd., Suite 101
Brampton, Ontario
Canada L6T 4J5
(905) 459-1481
www.cca-afc.com
> Cat Fanciers Association (CFA)
P.O. Box 1005

Important Note
> Immunizations and de-worming of your kitten are essential, so as not to endanger any people or fellow animals.
> Since some cat diseases and parasites can be transmitted to humans, a veterinarian should be consulted in case of uncertainty.
> Anyone with cat allergies should consult a medical practitioner before getting a kitten.
> General liability insurance may protect against damages caused by cats—ask your agent.

Manasquan, NJ 08736
(732) 528-9797
www.cfainc.org
> Cat Fanciers Federation (CFF)
Box 661
Gratis, OH 45330
(937) 787-9009
www.cffinc.org
> National Cat Fanciers Association (NCFA)
10215 West Mount Morris Road
Flushing, MI 48433
(810) 659-9517
www.nationalcatfanciers.com/info.html
> The International Cat Association (TICA)
P.O. Box 2684
Harlingen, TX 78551
(956) 428-8046
www.tica.org
> Traditional Cat Association, Inc. (TCA)
18509 N.E. 279th St.
Battle Ground, WA 98604
www.traditionalcats.com/
> United Feline Organization (UFO)
P.O. Box 3234
Olympia, WA 98509-3234
(360) 438-6903
http://unitedfelineorganization.org/

Miscellaneous Organizations and Agencies

> American Humane Association
63 Inverness Drive East
Englewood, CO 80112-5117
(303) 792-9900
fax (303) 792-5333
> American Society for the Prevention of Cruelty to Animals (ASPCA)
424 East 92nd Street
New York, NY 10128
(212) 876-7700

Insurance

Contact your personal insurance company for details.

Registration

Contact your local animal welfare organization; some areas do not require cat registration.

Books

> Bessant, Claire. *The Cat Whisperer.* Barron's Educational Series, Inc., Hauppauge, New York, 2002.
> Davis, Karen Leigh. *The Cat Handbook.* Barron's Educational Series, Inc., Hauppauge, New York, 2000.
> ———. *The Everything Cat Book, 2nd Edition.* Adams Media, Massachusetts, 2007.
> Helgren, J. Anne. *Encyclopedia of Cat Breeds.* Barron's Educational Series, Inc., Hauppauge, New York, 1997.
> Ludwig, Gerd. *300 Questions About Cats.* Barron's Educational Series, Inc., Hauppauge, New York, 2007.
> Wegler, Monika. *A Kitten's Life.* Barron's Educational Series, Inc., Hauppauge, New York, 2005.

Photo References

All photographs in this book were taken by Monika Wegler, with the exception of: Arco Digital/Steimer, Christine: p. 22; Ardea/Labat Jean-Michel: back cover (left), p. 16; Axmann, Christine: p. 2 (right), p. 64 (left); BIOS/Herent Sébastien: back cover (center); Juniors Tierbildarchiv: p. 24, p. 57-3 (Monika Wegler); mauritius images: p. 2 (Arthur Cupak), p. 3 (age fotostock), p. 42 (photo researchers), p. 48 (photononstop); plainpicture/Schneider, R.: p. 54; WILDLIFE/S. Muller: p. 4.

The Author

Brigitte Eilert-Overbeck has been an enthusiastic cat hobbyist for many years. She has studied the behavior of these fascinating animals intensively. In the German TV series *Hören und Sehen* (Hearing and Seeing) she held the portfolio "Frau und Familie" (Woman and Family). She has also written numerous articles on the subject of pets and several books on cats, as well as articles for cat magazines.

The Photographer

Monika Wegler is one of the best pet photographers in Europe. In addition, she is also successful as a journalist and animal book author. Further information is available from www.wegler.de/englisch/start.htm.

SOS—What to Do?

Rescue action

PROBLEM: Your kitten has climbed in to a tree and cannot get down. It is frightened and "meows" continuously.

SOLUTION: Place a ladder against the tree close to the kitten...and keep calm. Sooner or later the kitten will gather sufficient courage to climb down on its own.

Aggression

PROBLEM: The kitten responds to your attempts to pet it with bite and scratch attacks.

SOLUTION: Play with the kitten to (re)gain its trust; games with the play fishing pole are particularly suitable for that purpose. Always talk to your kitten; before picking it up let it smell your extended hand first. No sudden, violent movements!

Bad table manners

PROBLEM: The kitten regularly turns its feeding place into a battlefield.

SOLUTION: Check the food bowls; they should be shallow and have a large diameter. Nearly all cats dislike it when their whiskers come into contact with the edge of the bowl.

Scratch attacks

PROBLEM: Although the kitten is actively using its scratching post, it also keeps attacking the sofa or other furniture.

SOLUTION: When neither a detour back to the scratching post nor a shower from the spray bottle works, set up an additional scratching post. There are inexpensive models made of corrugated cardboard that need to be replaced occasionally but are popular with cats. Upholstered sofa arms and backrests that are vulnerable to scratching can be wrapped in aluminum foil. This may look strange, but this is one of those materials cats do not like to feel under their paws. Instead, they will go to the new post.

Offender

PROBLEM: The kitten uses the flower bowls on the balcony as a cat box.

SOLUTION: Scatter a generous amount of ground pepper over the soil in the flower bowl and pots, because cats tend to sniff before they squat down to do their business. Alternately, place large gravel stones or strips of aluminum foil over the soil; it is difficult to dig among them.